A Grand Land

Noel Hodgson

The Reiver Press
The Old School House
Tillmouth
Cornhill-on-Tweed
TD12 4UT

First published in Great Britain by The Reiver Press, 2012

www.noelhodgson.co.uk

A CIP catalogue record for this book is available from the British Library.

ISBN 978-0-9545181-2-7

Printed and bound in Great Britain by The Billingham Press

I wish to dedicate *A Grand Land* to the memory of **Fred Dyson**, of Alnwick, whose teaching and friendship further inspired me to appreciate words, their meanings – and beyond.

Also, special thanks to:
David White, *editor* and Bill Grisdale, *designer*.

For reading and selecting the poems they liked:
Claire Bagness, Gerald Dickinson, George Gibson, Judith Hodgson, Lizzie Sharp, Emma Whittingham.

All accompanying photographs by Noel Hodgson, except:
Robynne Hodgson *'Departed'*; H Benicce *'Snowballing'*;
Kevin Dowling *'Shores Of Youth'* and *'Winter Daffodil'*;
Bill Grisdale *'Summer In March'* and *'Tom's Kingdom'*;
and Kevin Temple *Rear cover image*.

Following in the footsteps of my two previous collections of poetry, *Below Flodden* and *Dancing Over Cheviot*, I have attempted once more to celebrate the experience of growing up and living a life here in Northumberland.

In *A Grand Land*, people, places and events are portrayed as I perceive them, with affection and understanding. Photographs accompany some of the poems, and all have brief explanations regarding their creation. The poems are varied in content and style. I hope that the reader enjoys them and can share in the delight of this remarkable corner of northernmost England.

At a time of my life when loss is more frequent, I make no excuse for expressing it, with or without sentiment. Still, however, I am indebted to a life of fortune – and to family, friends and readers for their encouragement.

contents

A Fisherman's Life

At the river's side,
The old fisherman
Feels the sun's joy
Leaning on his shoulder.

Squinting at the ripple
Creasing the water's palm,
His hands anticipate
The thrill of capture.

The rod jolts,
His arms flex;
Winding in and out,
His face taut as the line.

The fish writhes,
A dazzling, curved shadow,
Arching clearly above
The sparks of splash.

Diligently,
The old fisherman
Plays out the strength
Of the fighting salmon.

Near the edge,
A tiny floating branch
Brushes the fish's snout,
Releasing the hook.

As his catch darts away,
His mind reels back;
Barbed wire, cruelty, hunger,
The faint hope of escape.

A smile strokes
His glazed cheek;
The warm caress
Of mercy's tender kiss.

Despite a major effort, ninety-four-year-old Henry McCreath, from Berwick, suffered bad luck, failing to land this huge salmon. Henry, a survivor of a Japanese P.O.W. camp, was typically philosophical about his loss.

A Gathering

My dog and I
Walk out in the late evening,
Turning off the country road
Towards Stickle Heaton farm.

Silently, we slip
Into a dark wood.
I seek a fallen branch;
She noses the ground,
Hunting animal spoor.

Shouldering a log,
I make my way home,
Seeing no one.

Trailing behind, the dog
Carries a snatch of scents
She can warm to later,
Asleep by the hearth,
As they fizzle and crackle
In fireside dreams.

I began this poem without ambition.
A small trinket of an outing on a late June's
balmy evening turned into a portrait, of sorts,
for memory's mantelpiece.

A Grand Land

Felled by a huge bale,
Cameron lay semi-conscious.
When the loader freed him
He rolled over and passed out.

In hospital recovering,
His mind was on the harvest;
How they'd cope back home.

News of his accident
Bolted across the countryside
Like a herd of bullocks.
The phone rang and rang,
Farmers and folk anxious for him,
Offering their help.

That's what's good about here;
People knowing people,
Neighbours ready and willing
To do what they can –
To lend a hand,
To be of use.

It's this concern and feeling
For others that makes it
A grand place to live;
A land of fellowship
And kinship;

Northumberland.

Lucky to survive, Cameron Binnie from Tillmouth was strong enough to recover and, after months of treatment, he returned to work. During his absence, his family, through effort and pride and help from others, worked their socks off to maintain the business.

An Awful August

Day after day, driving rain sleeting down:
Rivers bloated, thick brown as gravy,
Churning, breaking banks, dragging off
A haul of bushes, trees, debris, drowned sheep;
Sodden fields runnelled with water,
Crops soaked and wasting, heads drooped;
Huge pools sinking roads and tracks;
The landside, drenched and dishevelled,
Shabby as a mud-ditched blanket.

In the farmhouse kitchen he clutches
A mug of steaming tea, staring at it blankly.
She, keeping busy, ironing at the table.
The window buzzes with another downpour.

She passes him a picture postcard
From Mallorca: sun, sea and sand.
"It's from Chris and Pat," she says.
"Piss and Crap," he mutters.
She pauses and smiles thinly.
"Not lost your sense of humour, then."
He shrugs, rises, giving her a mild, weary grin.

She hears him in the hallway,
Shuffling into his coat and Wellington boots.
Shortly, she spots him through the sprayed glass,
A blurred figure, shambling across the farmyard.

She tugs another garment down from the rail
Suspended from the ceiling above the stove,
And thumps the iron down with vehemence,
Relieving the silent scream battened down
Beneath the grievance of a sigh.

August, 2008: continual rain with few breaks. Miserably, for over a month ripe fields of corn awaited harvesting. The countryside looked grim and downcast, with the farming community feeling desperate and depressed; spirits strained by a foreboding of ruin and disaster, to be etched into folklore.

Berryhill

Past the old,
Stone farmstead
And a lone hen clucking,
A blue tractor spraying
A field of oats.

Below
The crag's face,
A fresh, green meadow,
Brown cattle lounging.

Across the skyline,
The Cheviot hills
Lazing in calm,
Morning light.

A brief
Enchantment,
Worthy of a thousand words,
Made everlasting,
By merely
These few.

A quiet, pensive morning in which the mind roams
like a lost child. As a Jane Siberry song goes, 'Love
is everything'. The beauty and serenity of this scene
stirred my affections and memories.

Another Night

Another night strewn with stars.
Another moon.
Another gate to lean on,
To marvel at snow-sheathed fields.

In local news,
Cars spinning off slippery roads
At Mousen Bends, Corby Crags,
Charlton Mires, Broome Park,
Kilham Brae, Crawley Dene;
No one badly hurt.

Reports from Afghanistan;
Another roadside bomb,
Another young soldier killed:
The thin-iced joy of Christmas.

Noel, Noel:
Another chance for hope and peace,
Another prayer – goodwill to all men;
A'men.

It's hard to separate the visionary from the
real world; the events that repeatedly stir our
conscience from the dream.

Battle Of Halidon Hill

Across the hillside before his troops,
Young King Edward, tall and proud
With hair, red-gold, shining like a crown,
Exhorts his army to lift their hearts,
Their nerve, their cheer, and win the day
With glorious might.

Over the vale, on Witch's Knowe,
Sir Archibald Douglas with greater force,
Delays his attack, waiting for the tide
To fill the Tweed, so after the battle,
The English, vanquished, will not escape
When put to flight.

But first, for honour and chivalry,
Turnbull, a giant Scot, meets Benhale,
England's champion; though a smaller man,
With slashing sword the Norfolk knight
Swiftly slays both Turnbull and his dog,
In a one-sided fight.

Undeterred by this sorry presage,
The Scots, dismounting, begin their advance
Through marshy bog, and heavy-legged
As they slog closer, are easy targets
For English archers, who aim crossfire
From left and right.

Under this rake of scalding arrows,
The slaughter continues; the Scottish ranks
Rapidly crumble in pitiful waves.
Even Archibald's surge, to break through
To Berwick, meets with disaster.
And though many, like Lord Ross,
Fight nobly to their deaths, others who flee
Are cruelly pursued by English riders,
Until out of sight.

After the rout, the field's ghastly show,
And now with the siege finally over,
King Edward, victorious, rides into town
To restore it once more to England's rule;
While his Queen, safe at Bamburgh,
Rejoices at the news, the wail of widows
Swings over the Lowlands, up through
The Glens, like a vixen's howl on a bleak,
Lonely night.

The battle of Halidon Hill, 19 July 1333, was as disastrous for Scotland as was Flodden in 1513. In both conflicts the Scottish advance was stifled by boggy ground, but here, English bowmen inflicted most carnage. The tactics employed by King Edward's army later served him well, at Crécy and Poitiers, against the French.

After the siege, Berwick remained in English hands until 1462, when the Scots regained it for a final twenty years.

Bowden Doors

Easy to reach from the road,
A dozen climbers spread along the crag
Tackling named routes: 'The Runnel',
'Robber's Rib', 'Bloody Nose', 'Runt',
And many others, each listed, described,
Difficulty and skill graded.

Passionate men and women attached
To the geometry of moorland sandstone.
Limbs stretching, pulling, pushing,
Probing their way, fingers and toes
Fondling the wall in search of grip.

A startling, sunny, blessed Easter Sunday.

Adventurers on the loose across this corner
Of northernmost England: climbers, ramblers,
Cyclists, horse riders, canoeists, orienteerers,
Each activated, inspired by Nature's hold,
Summoning and challenging them to feel
Through stillness of heart and mind
The power imbued in this spare, rippling,
Solitary land, enshrined by faith and survival.

Despite the climbs being short, the cliff offers
exciting, challenging routes for climbers of varied
experience, and are very popular. From the moor's
summit the view of North Northumberland can be
stunning. In this poem I attempted to link Easter's
religious importance with the dedication of these
outdoor followers.

Daft Lads

Derek,
Like Roger,
Gone from me.
Pals at school – daft lads,
We laughed and played
And enjoyed our youth,
Then grew to be men,
To love and marry.

We each had two;
A boy and girl –
Two boys –
A girl and boy!

Derek, eyes closed,
Slipped away from his
Suffering, with stoicism:
Roger is another story.

Only by chance
Have I outlived them;
Only by good fortune,
Did I know them well.

Looking for an old poem, I accidently came across an unfinished version of another – this one, written 22 June 2007. Perhaps it was too early after Derek's passing for me to be able to complete it, but I'm pleased it wasn't lost. And so, I caught my breath and faced it again.

Departed

Horses galloping
Along the beach;
A man with a dog;
Two women strolling
Side by side.

A single ship
Perched on the horizon.

Later,
We talk about
The elegance of horses,
The benefit of dogs,
And intrigue of women
Together – happy,
Outside the scope
Of men;
Alone.

A quiet winter beach
near Bamburgh, with
images that stoked
thoughts which grew,
reaching deeper into
a soulful self.

17

Fred

Alone,
He stays up nights,
Exploring thoughts,
Wishing to express
How science and feeling
Are united in a love
For things visible,
Invisible.

Silently,
He stays up late,
Seeking to describe
With solid, fluent lines
An intricate world,
Connecting forces
Of invention, craft,
Nature.

Keenly,
He remains awake
Attempting to reveal
The wonderment
Of life's experience –
Its designs and concepts –
Beyond heavenly
Terms.

Fervently,
He pursues ideas,
Growing and learning
Along wisdom's long,
Arduous highway,
Enchanted by
Its endless
Beginnings.

Avidly,
He remains alert,
Mining knowledge
To illuminate the magic
Of stars, moon, sun,
Eclipsing his darkness,
With numinous
Light.

Fred Dyson of Alnwick, a devotee of literature and science, has inspired my own writing for over forty years. Late at night, alone, Fred, although blind, finds he is able to pursue his quest for awareness with a spirit of adventure and freedom. The phrase 'endless beginnings' in my poem alludes to Fred's utmost regard for T.S. Eliot's poetry.

I wrote this a year before Fred died, 13 August 2011.

George Neighbour

"Has anyone seen George? He's nowhere to be seen!"
The words fly like swallows across the village green.
George is on the wander, visiting folks here and there;
A troubadour, a minstrel, a harlequin – a timeless kind
Of a bloke, seeming without a care.

My, how he enjoyed good company, to be surrounded
By a friendly crowd, particularly at parties,
Where he appeared so pleased, so proud;
Restless as a peacock, he'd strut and hover
And waltz about the room, his big smile beaming
Like a glorious, quarter moon.

Oh, that mighty grin! Eyes crackling, a sparkle
Of sheer joy! A lantern of happiness, swaying,
Weaving exuberantly between us with lustre and vim.

And then, what clothes he adorned himself in!
A rainbow in motion before our very eyes;
So dapper, so jaunty, so trim! An extravagance
Of style and colour, only George could realise,
Turning heads, making us smile.

Indeed, he was vaudeville, he was theatre,
Played 'Town Crier' each year at Alnwick Fair;
A role he performed naturally, with zeal, panache,
And customary flair.

No matter where, George loved a stage, openly
Displaying a boyish yearning to be free; a dining table,
A bar, a concert hall, a dance floor – all close to his heart!

Do you remember how he used to dance, instinctively,
Hands in pockets, at any music he heard?
A shuffle, a jig, a skip, a prance, stepping
And spinning merrily, free as a bird!

Yes, we can all remember his passion for dance,
For art and food and wine, each spiced by a sense
Of occasion – a notion of romance.

With his swarthy looks and Latin features,
How he adored the Mediterranean isles –
Their dazzling landscape, bays and beaches.
How his childlike zest for the sun and the continental
lifestyle made him feel so much at ease and relaxed,
Far from the winter of our modern-day demands
That caused him worry and strife.

So, let's remember George as we knew him best,
Believing in others, perhaps more than himself;
Happy, smiling, affable – a fun-loving guy;
Bejewelled, vivid, gaudy – a bright butterfly!

But now, alas, his star will no longer roam,
Down the road or lane or path to our homes.
No more will the cry echo round the village square;
"Has anyone seen George? He's nowhere to be seen –
He's disappeared somewhere!"

I read this eulogy at George's funeral service
at Felton – a service befitting the sparkle of
a fun-loving man.

Grace Darling

7 September 1838, the
steamer 'Forfarshire',
having lost power
through boiler failure
was blown back in a
storm and struck the
Big Harcar rock. Eleven
survivors managed
to clamber onto the
rock but two children
perished before
William Darling, the
Longstone Lighthouse
keeper, with his
daughter, Grace,
rowed to the rescue.
The disaster, in which
forty-three were
drowned, was widely
reported, and Grace's
courage was nationally
honoured. Genuinely,
she was embarrassed
by the fuss and
adulation she received.
Here I imagined how
modestly she might
have played down her
part in the rescue.

Grace Darling died
of tuberculosis,
20 October 1842,
aged only twenty-six.

"I didn't think much about it
At the time.
My brother wasn't there
So I had to help m' dad.
We had to do what we could
For the poor people
Stranded on the rock.

Afraid?

Well, w' were anxious,
But dad was determined,
And luckily I was there
To help him.
It was only later when folks
Started talkin', did w' know
How important it was.

Fame?

Me, being a woman,
A lot was made of it.
But it was m' dad
That did the most.
It was him that knew how
To reach them an' what to do.
I only rowed the one time."

Holy Island

Anchored off shore,
Like the deck of a huge ship,
The island, surrounded by sea,
Lies dormant in the morning haze,
Awaiting the invading, visiting hordes,
Once the road-crossing surfaces
Like a drowned arm.

Centuries ago,
Lowered from heaven
With its cargo of new faith,
Monks distributed its goods
Across this northern land;
Righteous travelling salesmen,
Freely offering the riches of its bounty –
Hope, peace, the love of a forgiving God.

And even today, moored offshore,
Like a venerable museum spectacle,
The great vessel still holds
Among its many souvenirs
A gift no one can buy, only earn;
The inner words that whisper help,
Towards a stronger, gentler state
Of being.

The sanctity and influence of Lindisfarne in the history of the Church brings thousands of visitors each year. The aura of early Christendom can be anticipated in the semi-isolation of the island, as well as in the Priory's ruin. From the hill above Fenwick, the sight of it this particular day, ethereal and serene, prompted the image of the poem.

Homecoming

Beyond my room,
In the garden,
A group of farm people:
Two men and a woman, smoking.
In her arms she holds a child.
Other children, nearby,
Play with a small dog.

It is a dry, sunny evening,
And a tractor comes bumping
Down the hill.

There is a contentment
About these folk here
That is enviable.
The life they inhabit
Appears easy to bear;
Company, children, chat,
Gardening, smoking,
The joy of tractors
Coming home.

There are times when being alone seems to bring
you closer to that world around you of which you
are not a part.

Land Unbelonging

Above the Tweed, on the north side,
A fist of stony, boggy hinterland,
Held aloft by England since 1482.
Barren, weather-torn terrain,
Fit for swine, intrigue, murder,
Protecting Berwick's township;
Out of range from Scottish spear,
Arrow, sling or early cannon.

Claimed, defended, knuckled ground,
To thwart an enemy's bitter gaze,
Espying territory, naturally theirs.

For some five miles, I hike the border line,
Scotland to the left, England on my right,
All the way to the cliff-locked shore
And the remains of an end wall, below,
Feeling this tiny clasp of Northumberland,
Estranged, and to me, solely unbelonging.

This most northerly tip of England, known as
Berwick Bounds, is a relatively forlorn part of
Northumberland. The natural border here is the
River Tweed, but as maps show, the line deviates
to create a buffer zone of land meant to safeguard
Berwick during earlier times, from Scottish attack
and repossession.

It was here that the Battle of Halidon Hill, 1333,
resulted in a Scottish defeat as weighty and dire
as Flodden in 1513.

Learning

Years ago, when Dad scaled the wall
Of Craster Harbour and dived headlong
Into the sea, it was the talk of the countryside.

When brother Jim was banned from driving,
And bought a horse to transport himself
To and from the Craster Arms at Beadnell,
Locals shook their heads and grinned.

At the Bird Cage on Fenkle Street, Alnwick,
I vividly remember watching her dance,
Mesmerised by the slender sway of her figure,
And how desperate I felt to befriend her,
To have her hold my hand as we sat together,
Surrounded by smiles of admiration.

To my credit, I learned the hard way;
Having cold feet never warms the heart
And, however much you flap your wings,
You won't leave the ground without a spring.

the
bird
cage
club
Alnwick
Blacksbuildings, Fenkle Street

Sometimes a lack of confidence, and perhaps nerve, made growing up harder. The saying, "Shy bairns get nowt!" is one, in the vernacular, that sticks in my mind.

Lion Bridge, Alnwick

At the kissing gate
Beside the bridge,
A young couple
Linger to embrace.

In their arms
They hold the hope
Of early love;
Their lips pressing,
Breathing the breath
Of each other's yearning.

Together, united,
Bonded by a spirit
Strained from bloodlines
More ancient and mightier
Than the history
Of any castle or bridge,
They pass through,
Moving onwards,
Following the current
Of the time-filled river,
Hearts emblazoned
By their legacy
For joy and growth.

I saw this young couple
at the gate against the
ancient backdrop of
castle and bridge.
Our family trees stretch
back thousands of
years and the course of
our ancestral journeys
is staggering.
But, naturally, the
young, excited by
illusions, tend to look
towards the future,
wishing to create their
own history.

Mugger's Loan

Stretching along the upper fields, the lane
Crawls between fringes of tangled thorn.

Now little used, except for the occasional
Hiker, horse rider and farm vehicle,
The bridleway lies lorn and wasted.

Yet once, a highway where travelling folk
Made their home, camping in summer;
A site enlivened by wood fire, voices,
Sniffing dogs and the shuffle of ponies.

Evening: logs burning, men squatting, smoking;
Children at play, tossing stones at a branch;
Down by the burn, lads ferreting rabbits;
Amidst a huddle of tents, chattering women
Peeling potatoes and turnips for the pot.

An offspring of talk from yesterday's Fair:
How an old woman, boastful of her fine legs,
Hoisted up her skirt to show them to all;
On the cobbles, two drunks fighting like bears,
Clobbered by 'hornies' before hauled off to jail.
And wall-eyed Willie, selling his stolen vessels,
A gully knife in his belt to warn away thieves.

So here, the lane's name a tribute to them,
Their story of survival, their crafts and skills;
A hardy, independent, guarded community,
Protective and loyal to family, their freedom,
Their desire to exist beneath a dominant sky.
Their lives spirited from above, by ancestors
Watching over them, keeping a steadfast eye,
Holding them to a wandering, uncollared life,
Alongside nature's twists and turns.

The history of Gypsies is clouded in mystery and legend. Locally, Kirk Yetholm was an important base for a number of families. Due to prejudice, their influence is not generally appreciated. However, many local dialect words stem from the Romany language, e.g. 'Gadge' – man, 'Ladge' – embarrassed, 'Shan' – bad, 'Hornies' – police, and are still used around Berwick. It seems appropriate for the bridleway between Cramond Hill and Melkington to be named after them.

Mum

She walks with me, still,
Stick in her hand,
A gleam in her eye,
A fair, steady pace.

Looking up to the sky
I can picture her face,
Her slight, wondrous smile;
And my heart sings out,
For she walks with me, still,
Enjoying the views,
As I faithfully follow,
Mile after mile,
Along roads
We knew.

Each time I visited, I made a point of driving
her out into the countryside and stopping for
us to walk and view the farmlands she loved.
Her appreciation shone and her memories
filled her mind like gifts. I think of her often as
I walk alone, appreciating the loveliness of our
homeland and the love she gave.

Night Of The Axe

Stopping on the way, at Netherton's 'Star',
I sit drinking a pint, chatting with Vera,
When a holiday couple enters, eyes agog.
They ask politely for 'gin and tonic'.
Vera replies she's none: just wine, only white.
Glasses filled, they gaily join us in the room.
We talk of the area and where they've been;
They've visited Alnwick, pronouncing the 'l'.

At Rothbury, I hardly get through the door
When Musky is desperate to show me the axe
He'd bought for nine pounds at the Auction Mart.
Sanded, sharpened, painted and polished,
It gleams in his grip, like a work of art.
Paint on his hand, he's as proud as a bantam cock.

In the 'Newcastle House' we meet up with Richard.
"Don't mention the bloody axe," he insists.
I swear, Musky blinks, his face crumpling –
The creative fingers still stained with varnish.

Up at the 'Turk's Head', tall Thomas serves us.
We sit beside Maggie and two of her friends.
I enthuse about my glider flight that afternoon
From Milfield up above the College Valley.
How peering down I felt like a snooper.
Musky yawns and troops off to play Pool.

Joining them later, I challenge Richard.
I almost have him beaten when he plays,
"The best three shots I've ever made in my life."
Back at Jim's house and 'one for the road',
I ask for a lager but he says he hasn't any.
Sipping whisky together, he purrs again, gloating
Over the axe lying on the chair beside him.
I suggest he could sell it for ninety pounds.
His gaze glistens: "I certainly will not."

The next day, he assures me on the phone
That he couldn't see himself ever selling it.
"Not for ninety pounds," he proffers.

Jim Musk's delight at buying the axe cheaply, and
transforming it into something special, preoccupied
him totally. On the pool table, Richard Hutton
proved to be invincible. It was a night of extremes,
worth remembering.

Pieman Of Heighley Gate

Parked in the lay-by,
A blue chuckwagon;
On its sides, slogans
And a hefty menu inviting
Trail riders to pull up,
Rest their mounts,
Grab a bite.

Dave, amiable cook,
With his western-style
Haircut and moustache,
Readily greeting every
Cowboy and cowgirl
With cheerful courtesy.

Over a dozen years
His reputation has grown;
He's the Pie Man,
The Snack Boss,
Known throughout
The territory;
Quick on the grill,
Fast on food,
Jokes for free.
From sunrise to sundown,
Five days a week,
A servant to service.

On the high plain
Above the Wansbeck River,
Cook and kitchen
Providing a welcome break,
Warmth of conversation
And homely refreshments
For saddle-weary drivers,
On their arduous, sometimes
Lonesome journeys
Across this wild,
North land.

Opposite Heighley Gate Garden Centre the blue van (now black) is a common, almost permanent fixture. More out of curiosity than hunger, I stopped one morning and was impressed by the bacon roll and Dave's cordial nature, hinged with humour. For me, being a cowboy fan, his image fitted the role of chuckwagon cook, hence my slanted praise of him as a popular, regular guy.

ITER

		£1.20
	Mince & Onion Pie	£1.30
	Steak Pie	£1.20
£1.70	Scotch Pie	£1.20
£1.90	Two Pork Pies	£1.30
£2.70	Chicken & Mushroom Pie	£1.95
	& Potato Pie	0.40
	(...den Peas)	£1.60

PIEMAN'S *GOB* BREAKER

ONIONS, A SQUARE SAUSAGE,
SLICES BACON AND MUSHROOMS IN
A LARGE BUN
£3.10

Road To Belford

Unshaven and solemn,
wearing tattered clothes,
He follows the road
wherever it goes.
There is no brightness
in his pace,
And his head is lowered
to hide his face.

Cars pass heedless,
he seeks no ride,
He knows there are none
that are on his side.
He knows no one cares
to inspect his grief,
For who in green summer
wants an autumn leaf?

I passed him without a care. It was easy
to do. He was abject and alone. But the
picture remained and asked to be studied.

Saved A Life

Spotted the struggle,
The helpless hump.
Braked hard.
(Checking the mirror first)
Stopped suddenly,
Jumped out the car,
Vaulted the fence,
(One hand on a post)
Raced over the field.
(Without pulling a muscle)

Desperately,
The ewe on its back
Pawed the air,
(As if drowning)
Its lamb standing alongside.
(A pathetic sight)

Heaving it over,
(Heavier than I thought)
She stumbled to her feet,
Paused, eyes glazed.
(I held her balance)
She staggered a few steps,
Stopped to pee, then wandered off.
(I've seen worse)

I watched them trail away,
The hungry lamb eager to suckle.
(I admitted a modest smile)
After all, it's not every day
You save a life!

Once you've shepherded you never lose that instinct to watch the flock! Here I ran to the rescue at White House farm, near Alnwick, but my passenger, a refugee from the city, believed I was acting oddly.

September 10th, 1513

On the forward slope of Branxton Hill
Where the Scottish army had assembled for battle,
Heron and his outlaws pause to gaze down
Upon the field of white, semi-naked corpses,
Where hundreds of figures tread carefully,
Plundering what remains to be found.

In the expanding, dazzling light of dawn,
The scale of carnage leaves them speechless,
Disbelieving of the many thousands killed,
All there below them, to be witnessed,
Like looking down upon a pale, long beach
Of washed-up bodies, drowned in death.

Impassively, 'Bastard' Heron sits on his horse,
While beside him, Straughen, Weatherburn,
Hedley, Telfer and Thompson stare blankly,
Never having experienced in their lives
Such a vast and terrible scene of slaughter.

"Jesus," a voice mutters in the column behind,
And the lone word leaves its trail in the air.

An extract from my novel, *Heron's Flight*, about
the battle of Flodden. Since the battle ended in
darkness the previous day, it was only the next
morning that the horrendous loss was reckoned,
numbering nearly fifteen thousand.

Snowballing

Through the night it had snowed heavily
So, leaving the car, I walked to work,
Taking care, of course, on the slippery surface,
But enjoying the clean, crisp air,
Which freshened my mood, my well-being.

Around me, the hills were papered white,
Heralded, perfectly, by a cloudless, blue sky.

Nearing the boys' school-yard,
There were screeches of thrill
And snowballs flying in all directions.
I waved a greeting at the nearest group
From where a snowball was thrown,
Just missing my head.

Well, how could I pretend to be offended,
And blunt their shining, merry faces,
When the morning had simply given us
A craving to be daring, to feel free?

A crisp, joyous morning to be experienced
equally, without divisions. I taught at Glendale
School, Wooler, from 1972 to 2006.
Days to remember.

Snowman

Snowman smiling in a snow-covered yard,
Stick arms extended in a careless gesture
To the flailing wind, and growing menace
Of gathering clouds.

Not so the sheep coughing at the fence,
Hunched in peril.

Warming his hands by the fireside,
The shepherd rises, crosses to the window
To glare at the sky.

Dutiful, he slips on jacket, coat, hat,
Socks and boots, to leave his cottage.

Stony-faced against the blast,
He trudges forward, head cowed.

Over Coldsmouth Hill a white blizzard swells,
Before pouring down Longknowe valley,
Like a tidal wave.

I remember one lambing night at Red Steads farm,
Howick, when forced to go outside to face the
storm with dread. But nothing like the challenge
faced by hill shepherds when duty calls.

Shores Of Youth

Above Newfield's rooftops
The sea, flat and still,
Smooth as a blue tablecloth;
Reminding me of shores,
My young life leaned upon…

Alnmouth: families filling
Bags with sea coal, donated by
The previous night's wild storm:
Pushing our bounty home
On heavy, loaded bicycles,
Jubilant of toil and gain.

Sugar Sands: flushed-faced,
Enjoying a game of football
With lads from Longhoughton;
Sitting on a bank, village girls
Watching, careless of the score,
Showing a cool interest.

Embleton: Emerging
From waves, like a sea nymph,
She runs up the beach to kneel
Down at my side, smiling.
Together, on the dune, aware,
Her long, wet hair gleaming.

Beadnell bay: fitness training;
Running along the tide's edge,
Pacing my shadow, each bound
Imprinted in the sand, spurring
Feelings of renewal and virtue;
Every heartbeat, an exaltation.

The shore below Greenhill:
Stepping with alertness over rocks,
Scrambling for words amid
Sounds of gush and flow; seeking
The fresh scrawl of line's rhythm
In a simple, plaintive voice.

Budle bay: sunset's languid,
Russet glow, shimmering across
The estuary's darkening mudflat,
Striping veins of wrack-weed
And lagging streams; the sun
Drooping, like the last apple
On a tree, holding its breath.

Waiting for children to arrive on the playing field at Saint Mary's First School, Berwick, I gazed thoughtfully towards the sea. The Northumberland shoreline was an important and constant feature during formative years. These images revive experiences that lie engrained within me.

Summer In March

Afire, bristling warmth,
The late March sunshine
Uplifting us, day after day.

Temperatures and hopes
Soar as we toast the glory
Of the Spring countryside.

Lambs basking in fields;
Green blades glistening;
Birds dancing in the trees.

Nothing but praise, until
Jimmy, seated along the bar,
Bemoans, "We'll pay for it."

Next week, freezing rain;
Sleet and perished lambs;
The Cheviots bloated white.

Near a flame-roaring hearth,
Jimmy, hunched on a stool,
Clutches his ale, amber-eyed.

March 2012, a mini-heat wave had us smiling and sitting outside, faces uplifted to feel the sun's warmth. The last thing we wanted was words of gloom, though wise they proved, with sleet and snow and freezing cold the following week. I suppose every pub has its woe-monger.

Surrey's March

We ride on bicycles to Flodden field,
Following the Earl of Surrey's route;
Unlike most of his 20,000 soldiers
Who trudged the journey on foot.

We are well fed, bright and happy
After a good night's restful sleep,
In soft beds, warm and comfortable –
Not on sodden ground, like sheep.

From Wooler Haugh to Barmoor,
Through Bowsden on past Duddo,
We consider his grim-faced army,
Rain-lashed, with their spirits low.

We cross the old bridge at Twizel,
Pedal on southwards to Pallinsburn;
Did some whisper of their fears,
Or were they bold, intrepid men?

Did they think about their families,
Of the love they left back home?
Did they march alongside friends,
Yet still feel wretched and alone?

Beyond Branxton we dismount,
Stride uphill towards the cross,
Where Scottish flags fly proudly,
Remembering their terrible loss.

And at once, we feel uneasy,
Standing solemn in silent dismay,
For the soldiers we have followed,
For the tribute that we've paid:

At this monument to both sides,
Where honour should be shared,
There is not one English flag raised
In memory of their dead;

Not a single English flag in sight
To commemorate our dead.

The monument, erected in 1910, was dedicated to the brave of both nations. On bicycles, Gerald Dickinson and I arrived at the site, late afternoon, 9 September 2009. The monument's message is simple enough for us all to repect. Surely one flag from each country would have been more fitting?

Terror On Court

Evening tennis
On a cinder court,
Sheltered by a tall,
Thick, surrounding hedge;
A jug of Pimm's waiting
For us on a cane table,
Amid deck chairs.

Thirty all,
Three-four down,
I'm preparing to serve
When our sheltered world
Is shaken by the sudden
Thunder of a fighter jet
Practising, low overhead.

Spontaneously,
We duck and cringe,
Deafened by the explosion
Of noise, before continuing
Our evenly-fought set.

Only later, drinks in hand,
Do we pause to pity
The desperate families
Of a far-off, war-torn country,
Cowering in frequent terror,
Of the strikes and volleys
Such brutes serve down;
All games to love.

'Nippers' is an affectionate term for pupils attending Loretto Junior School. The Nippers Tennis Club, formed circa 1947 by Old Lorettonians, Geoff McCreath and John Lindsay, meet at Tillmouth to play on Wednesday evenings throughout the summer. The shattering noise of the Tornado that evening reminded me of another occasion, on the playing field at Glendale School, Wooler, when the children recoiled in shock as an aeroplane hurtled past.

Staring At Stars

Leaves have tumbled,
Exposing trees
To frosty winds.

December is welcomed
By a whiskery full moon
And an icy handshake.

In the night's beam,
Sheep lie glassy-eyed,
Staring starwards.

Beside radiant flames,
A log basket heaped high,
Coal scuttle crammed full.

Rosily, the room's cosiness
Pulls us closer to the spell
Of winter leering in.

Winter's premature arrival in November 2010
caused consternation. The freezing conditions
lasted throughout December into the New Year.
It was scenic but grim, and keeping warm was
a challenge, reviving basic instincts for survival.

The Hurl Stone

"Ha!" shrieks the Devil on Cheviot's top,
As he hurls his spear towards Holy Isle.

"Aarrgh!" he howls, his face turned scarlet
In vile delight, watching it soar
Straight and true into a clear, blue sky.

"Death and destruction!" he shrills with ire,
"To fools who preach love across this land,
My terror rules!"

Towards the sea, upon Ros Hill,
A wandering monk, with heaven in his eyes,
Spots the missile and pierced by dread,
Clasps his hands in desperate prayer.

"Protect us Lord from this evil danger.
Save us," he implores, "from wicked death."

At once, appearing, a dark cloud swirls,
And a lightning bolt flashes, striking
And snapping the spear in two;
One end plunging into the River Till,
The other lancing a gentle hillside,
Like a huge spike.

Above Bizzle's crag, aghast in disbelief,
The giant Devil rages, and bounding madly,
Loses his footing, plummeting headlong
Into the jagged ravine, tumbling down,
'Til his skull smashes against a boulder,
And the echo of his screams is heard no more.

8

Across the vale upon Ros Hill,
The monk, transfixed, hails the miracle,
Before setting off to the mighty pillar,
There to kneel in praise of his Lord,
Avowing the stone should bear a cross,
And, forever, be attended; a symbol of warning
To the Devil's spite, and a lasting beacon
To God's merciful, infinite power.

The Hurl Stone, beside Chillingham Newtown was probably erected as an Anglican cross for local gathering of worship in early times. Another myth links it to spirits and fairies, with an underground passage between Cateran's Cave on Hepburn Moor and the Hen Hole on Cheviot. The Devil legend is more graphic and I wanted to verse it.

According to local farmer, John Jeffreys, the pillar was once taller, before sheared by lightning.

Winter Daffodil

A grey, November Saturday.
Spots of rain and chilly
Blades of wind skating down
Seahouses Main Street,
Raking through a handful
Of drab-looking shoppers,
Brushing shabby-feathered
Birds, hunched on rooftops.

She emerges from a doorway.

A young, blonde-haired woman,
Striking as a Calendar Girl,
Wearing gay-bright clothes;
A startling winter daffodil,
Gliding up the pavement
With a dazzling, sunny smile,
Before vanishing indoors,
Leaving her arms around us,
And the warm hug of summer,
To jolly us through the raw,
Lean-ribbed months ahead.

A surprising, heartwarming glimpse of a radiant,
attractive girl to bolster a dismal scene and
lighten hearts, wary of winter's approaching
footsteps.

Tom's Kingdom

Stepping down
From his caravan home
To pee into the hedge,
Tom, astride, is amazed
At the night's livid display;
Sparkling stars and moon
Flaring the countryside
In a festive glow.

Relishing its magnificence,
He is seized by an urge to cheer,
To run exuberantly through fields
And village, hooraying his delight,
Minstrelling his good fortune.

Laurelled by a leafy Autumn air,
The river's jingle, Tom returns inside
To peer between curtains
At the blueish sheen of outlined hills,
Cheviot, Hedgehope, Dunmore;
Mirthful, he imagines himself,
Like Orion, bounding across them.

Senses dazzled, shaken,
Tom wobbles back to his bed.
And elevated by the floating kingdom
Surrounding his palace walls,
He curls to sleep, snug as a cat,
With a twinkle of a smile.

Tom, a friend, told me of his thrill and his own amusing poem about the occasion. I also, on a late walk, had witnessed the glory of this dazzling November night. Not to be outdone, I wrote my own poem, enlarging his wonderment. Tom 'Cat', as some of us name him, has an adventurous, good humoured disposition with a leaning towards learning, care and joy.

"The world turns as it must."

(Mum's words to my son, Guy, in a dream)